Tricking Our Eyes

Dawn McMillan

Contents

What Dots?	2
Look at Lines	4
Move It!	8
Fun with Words	12
Picture This	14
Where Is It?	18
How Did They Do That?	22
Tricks of the Eye	23
Glossary	24

CW00842324

What Dots?

Sometimes we see things that are not there. Our eyes play tricks on us. They see one thing, but our brains tell us it is something else.

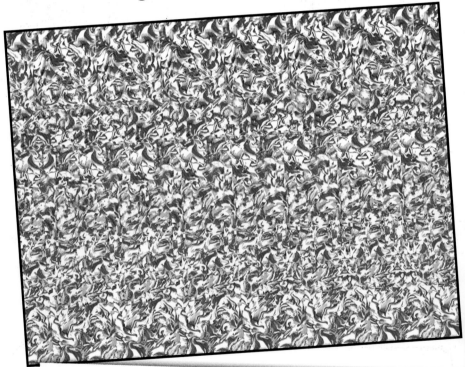

This is a Magic Eye picture. Stare into the picture. What can you see? Turn to page 24 to find out.

Look at this **pattern**.
Do you see some black dots?

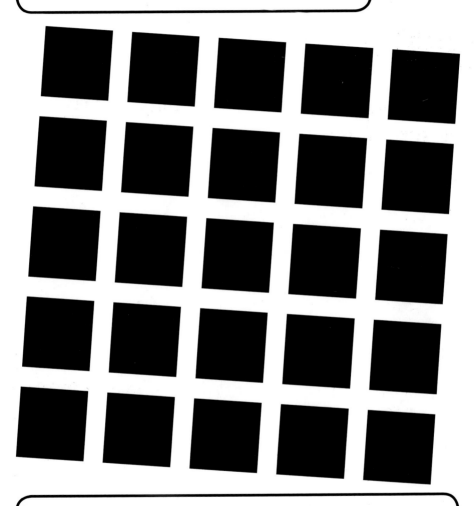

Look again. Can you count the dots?
Are they really there?
This is an **optical illusion**.

Now look at these lines.
Which is the shortest?
Which is the longest?

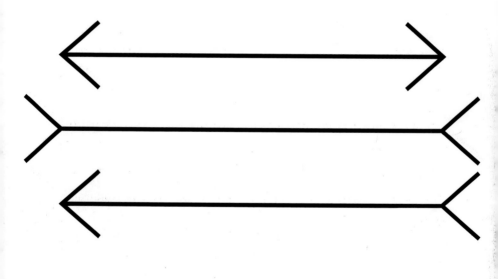

Look at the lines now.
They are all the same length.
Get a ruler and check!

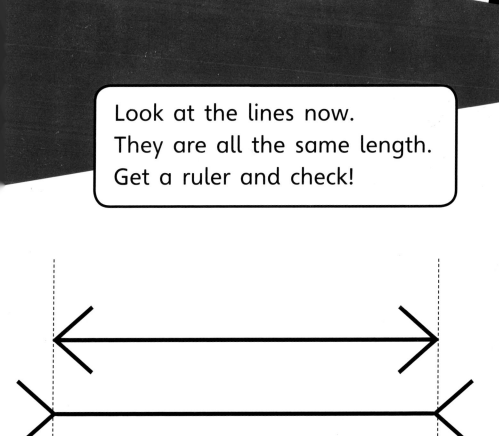

Look at these rows of rectangles. Do the rows look bent?

Believe it or not, the rows are not bent. They just look bent because of the way the rectangles are placed.

This famous illusion is now a building!

This optical illusion is on the floor of a shopping centre.

Move It!

Now try this:

1 Lie the book flat.

2 Look at the black dot in the middle.

3 Move your head closer.

4 Move your head back.

What happens?

The shapes seem to move because of the way they are placed.

Look at this pattern of shapes and colours.

As our eyes move across the picture, the wheels seem to turn.

The patterns of colour make us think we can see wheels moving.

Fun with Words

There are optical illusions made with words too.

Do you see two words in this picture?

Now try this one.

Read from left to right.
Say the colour of each word.
Don't say the word!

red blue orange purple

orange blue green red

blue purple red green

orange blue orange red

purple orange red blue

green red blue purple

orange blue red green

purple orange red blue

Picture This

Sometimes, you need to look more than once at a picture to see what is in it.

Look at this picture.
What do you see in the white space?
What do you see in the black space?

vase

heads

The white space shows a vase.
The black space shows two
heads looking at each other.

Can you see two different things in this picture?

This illusion first appeared on a German postcard in 1888.

Do you see the young girl or the old woman? Can you see both?

Now look at these pictures.
Show a friend. Did you both
see the same things?

Top picture 1: a duck and a rabbit
Bottom picture 2: a seal and a polar bear

17

Where Is It?

There are optical illusions in **nature** too. Many plants and animals use optical illusion for **camouflage**.

This photo shows a moth and leaves. Can you see the moth?

Here is the moth!

Now look at this photo. What do you think you are looking at?

If you said "rocks", you are only half right. You are also looking at plants.

Here are the plants!

These plants are called lithops, which means "like stone". They look like stone to stop animals from eating them!

How Did They Do That?

Some artists play tricks in their art.

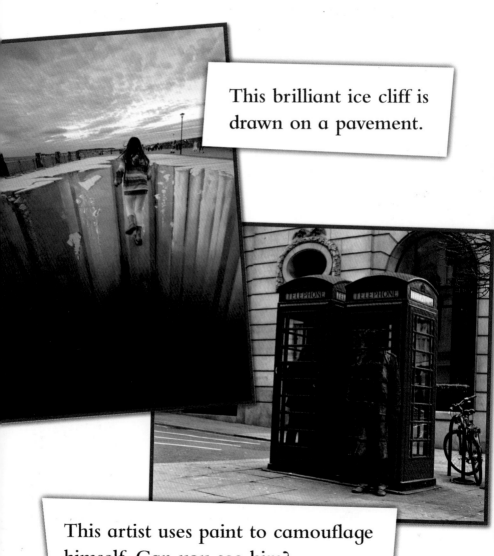

This brilliant ice cliff is drawn on a pavement.

This artist uses paint to camouflage himself. Can you see him?

Tricks of the Eye

Optical illusions are tricks of the eye and brain. What you see is not always as it seems ...

Glossary

camouflage — ways of blending in or becoming less visible

nature — the natural world, such as plants, animals or mountains

optical illusion — something we see that we think is real or true, but is not

pattern — things arranged in repeated ways

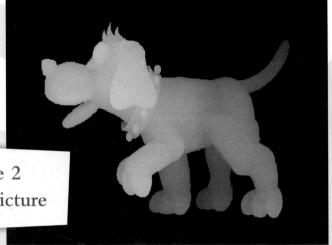

Answer: page 2
Magic Eye picture